KU-092-614

READY, STEADY, CODE!

CODING
with
Python®

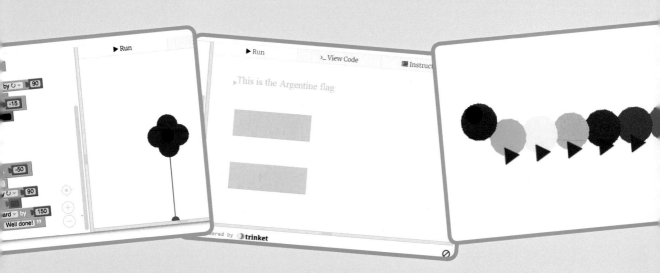

ÁLVARO SCRIVANO
ILLUSTRATED BY SUE DOWNING

First published in Great Britain in 2018 by Wayland
Copyright © Hodder and Stoughton, 2018
All rights reserved.
Editor: Hayley Fairhead

Design and illustrations: Collaborate
Wayland, an imprint of Hachette Children's Group
Part of Hodder & Stoughton
Carmelite House
50 Victoria Embankment
London EC4Y 0DZ

ISBN: 978 1 5263 0871 9
10 9 8 7 6 5 4 3 2 1

Printed and bound in China
An Hachette UK Company

www.hachette.co.uk
www.hachettechildrens.co.uk

The website addresses (URLs) included in this book were valid at the time
of going to press. However, it is possible that contents or addresses may
have changed since the publication of this book. No responsibility for any
such changes can be accepted by either the author or the publishers.

"Python" is a registered trademark of the Python Software
Foundation, used by Hodder & Stoughton Limited with permission
from the Foundation.

Trinket is available for free at trinket.io

CONTENTS

What is Python?

A programming language is a particular way to talk to a computer. It is a set of instructions that you give the computer to use. Python is a typed programming language that allows you to create animations, graphics and games. One of the advantages of Python is that you can get things done with less code than many other programming languages.

Many famous organisations, such as Google, YouTube, NASA and Yahoo, use Python. It has been used to produce the special effects for the *Harry Potter* and *Pirates of the Caribbean* films.

Trinket

All the projects in this book will be done using Trinket Blocks to create and run Python projects. This means you will not need to type the code, you can just drag, drop and snap the coding blocks together!

Note to parents

To use Trinket, go to: **https://trinket.io/**

Trinket allows your child to create and run Python projects in a web browser, on your desktop or on an iPad. In this book, the instructions assume the user is working on a desktop. There is no software to install. Children will be able to see their Python code and its output side-by-side. Children can also save their code online or share it with others with a link. Trinket Blocks is a free Trinket feature.

Creating Trinket accounts

Parental permission is required to create accounts for children under 13. It is recommended that a Trinket account be created by a parent or responsible adult.

Trinket can be used without downloading plug-ins or installing software. For your child to be able to save and share his or her projects, you will have to sign up and create a username and a password.

Trinket

These are the main features you will find when you open a new Trinket Blocks project:

Click here to run your program.

Save your work here.

Click here to view your Python program as text.

Menu

Project title

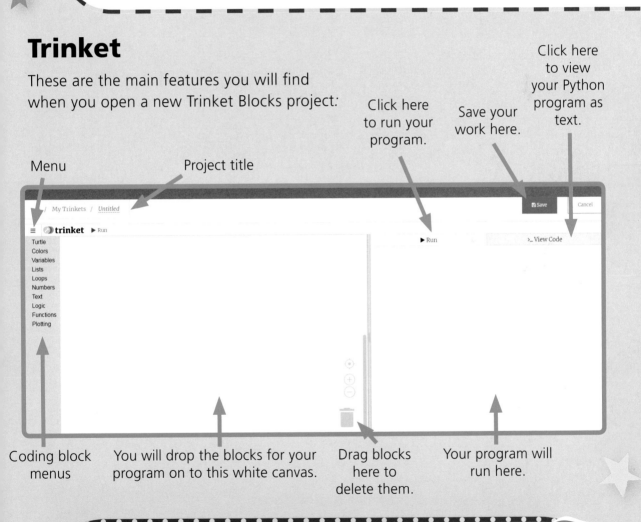

Coding block menus

You will drop the blocks for your program on to this white canvas.

Drag blocks here to delete them.

Your program will run here.

Be share aware

Usernames and passwords are personal information and, just like your toothbrush, YOU DO NOT SHARE THEM WITH ANYBODY!

TURTLE TALK
GET YOUR TURTLES CHATTING!

READY

In this project, you will use Python to create an animation of two turtles talking. Turtles are used in Python to show you the position of your program on the canvas.

Did you know?
Turtles have been on Earth since the time of the dinosaurs – over 200 million years ago!

1 GETTING STARTED
Go to Trinket: https://trinket.io/ and log in.

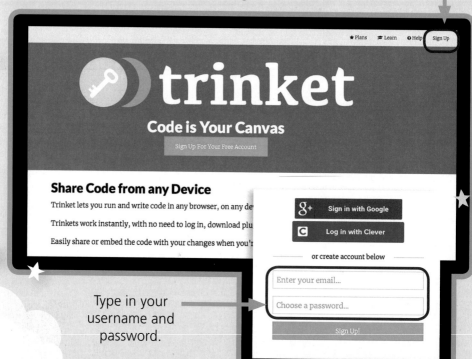

Type in your username and password.

STEADY

Now you've opened Trinket, it's time to begin a new program.

2 OPEN A NEW TRINKET

Click on **New Trinket ▼** and you will see the following drop-down menu. Click on Blocks.

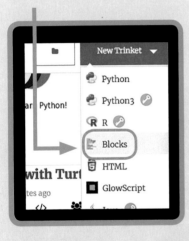

You will see the following window. Click on Turtle.

You will drop the blocks for your program in this white canvas.

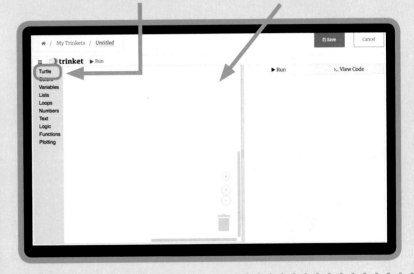

The following menu will open up on the right when you click on Turtle. Drag the **shape turtle ▼** block to the white canvas. You are now ready to code.

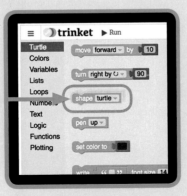

Did you know?

Both tortoises and turtles are reptiles: both lay eggs and have hard, bony shells. Tortoises have flatter backs than tortoises and they live on land, in deserts, grasslands and forests. Turtles have webbed feet for swimming and live in rivers, lakes or oceans.

Did you know?

Turtles have a hard shell that protects them like a shield. This upper shell is called a 'carapace'. Turtles also have a lower shell called a 'plastron'. Many turtle species can hide their heads inside their shells when attacked by predators.

CODE! ≫

Now you're ready to start programming your turtles.

If you select the wrong block, you can delete it by returning it to the blocks section on the left or dragging and dropping it in the bin in the bottom right-hand corner.

3 WRITE IN PYTHON

Add the following block from the Turtle menu and type: 'Hello! What are you doing?' inside the speech marks. Your program should look like this:

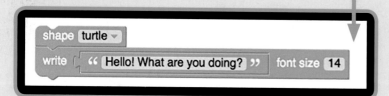

```
shape  turtle
write  " Hello! What are you doing? "  font size  14
```

Press ▶ Run to test your program. You should see your message disappearing off the right side of the screen, with a turtle overlapping the first word.

4 POSITION THE TEXT

Let's position the text towards the left of the screen. Add the `goto 0 , 0` block from the Turtle menu to your program, by clicking and dragging each block into the positions below. Change the numbers in the two purple blocks to: -50, 40.

Press ▶ Run to test your program. You should see the text on the right of the screen.

Did you know?

The common box turtle has a distinctive hinged lowered shell (the box) that allows it to completely enclose itself. It lives in woodlands, marshy meadows, floodplains, scrub forests and grasslands in much of the eastern United States.

5

USE THE PEN UP BLOCK

The turtle draws a line when it moves. To make the turtle move without drawing a line you need to use the `pen up` block from the Turtle menu. Your program should look like this:

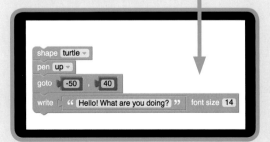

Press ▶ Run to test your program.

6 SET THE SPEED

Add a `speed 0` block to the program to make the turtle go faster.

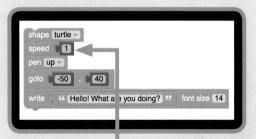

The number inside this block will set the turtle's speed. The higher the number, the faster the turtle will move.

Press ▶ Run to test your program.

7 USE A STAMP BLOCK AND SET THE PROGRAM'S COLOUR

A `stamp` block will produce an image of the character you are using in your program (a turtle), which is stamped on the white canvas.

Add a `stamp` and `set color to` block to your program, to make a stamp and colour it red. Add a further `goto 0 , 0` block to position the stamp.

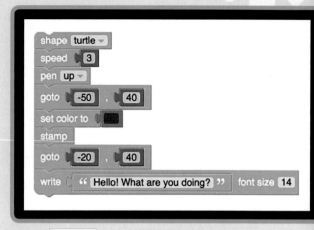

Press ▶ Run to test your program.

8 ADD ANOTHER TURTLE

Now you can add another turtle to talk to the first one. You need to make it look different to the first one, so you will need to use a different colour. Add the following blocks below the program in Step 7:

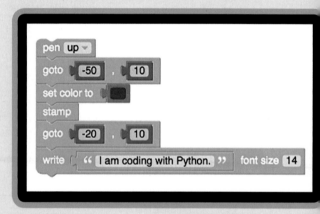

Press ▶ Run to test your program.

The `pen up` block can be snapped under the `write " " font size 14` block in the previous step or kept just below and separated.

Did you know?
The largest turtle is the leatherback sea turtle. It can weigh over 900 kg!

9 COMPLETE THE DIALOGUE

To complete the dialogue between the turtles, add the following blocks to your program:

You can right click on any block in the white canvas and copy it.

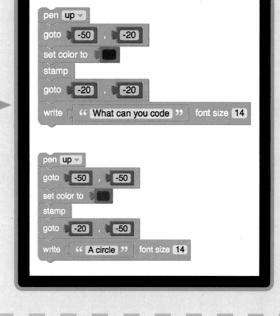

10 DRAW A CIRCLE

At the end of the dialogue, the blue turtle will draw a circle. Add the following blocks:

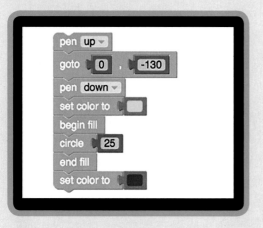

Press ▶ Run to test your program.

CHALLENGE

Add more lines to the program to make the turtles have a longer conversation.

🐢 Hello! What are you doing?
🐢 I am coding with Python.
🐢 What can you code?
🐢 A circle

🐢 Wow! That's great.
🐢 Thanks.

TROUBLESHOOTING

If you prefer the text centred, use the block to position the dialogue in the middle of your screen. Try -70 for your x co-ordinates.

ARGENTINA
CREATE THE FLAG AND DISCOVER SOME FUN FACTS ABOUT ARGENTINA!

READY >>

In this code, you will create the flag of Argentina by drawing different coloured rectangles.

1 **GETTING STARTED**
Go to Trinket: https://trinket.io/ and log in.

Type in your username and password.

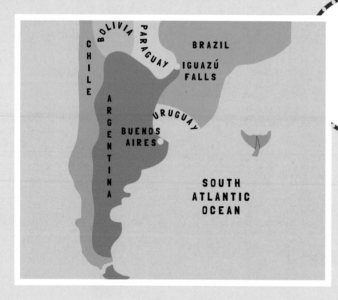

Argentina is the second largest country in South America after Brazil, and the eighth largest country in the world.

Did you know?
Lionel Messi was born in Rosario, Argentina. When he was 11 years old, he moved to Barcelona with his father. He now holds most of Barcelona's goal-scoring records and he is Argentina's all-time top scorer.

Did you know?
The name Argentina comes from the Latin word for silver: argentum.

Before you start coding, you need to open up a new Trinket.

2

OPEN A NEW TRINKET
Click on [New Trinket ▼] and click on Blocks.

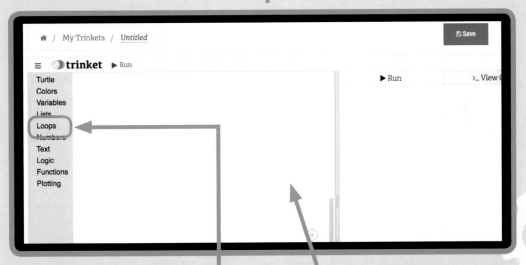

You will see the following window. Click on Loops.

You will drop the blocks for your program in this white canvas.

The following menu will open up:

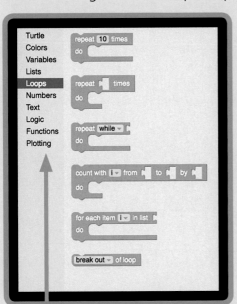

What is a loop?
A loop is a repeated command or set of commands. Loops repeat actions.

A different menu will open when you click on any of the other options on the left.

CODE! ➤➤

Now you need to create coloured rectangles to form your flag.

3

DRAW A RECTANGLE USING LOOPS

Add the following blocks to your program using the Loops and Turtle menus:

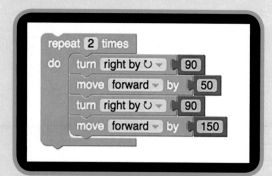

Press ▶ Run to test your program. You should see a rectangle on the right side of your screen.

4

COLOUR THE RECTANGLE

Add the following three blocks to the beginning and end of your program using the Turtle menu:

This block will set the colour of the program.

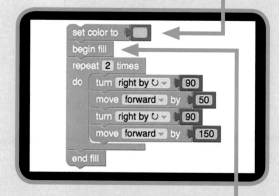

This block will colour the rectangle.

Press ▶ Run to test your program. You should see a blue rectangle on the right side of your screen.

Functions are like recipes. For example, to cook rice you have to follow a set of instructions: boil water, add salt, pour in the rice, simmer for 20 minutes, drain any remaining water and finally fluff the rice with a fork. Functions allow programmers to put all those instructions under one block and give it a name, such as 'Rice'. So, every time you need to make rice, you could use the function 'Rice'.

This is the name of the function.

5 CREATE A FUNCTION

The Argentine flag is divided into three horizontal rectangles, coloured blue, then white, then blue. Add the following block to your program, using the Functions menu:
Let's create a function by deleting 'do something' and naming the function 'Rectangle blue'.

From the Functions menu, add the function Rectangle blue that you have just created to the side of your program, like this:

Press ▶ Run to test your program. You should still see the same rectangle as in Step 4 but it is now a function and you will use it again in the next step.

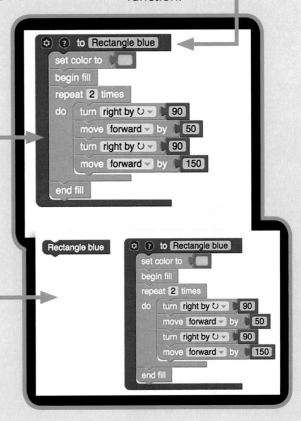

6 COPY A FUNCTION

Right-click on the block used at the start of Step 5 and select Duplicate.

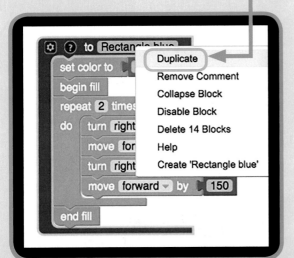

The Tango dance and music was created in Buenos Aires, Argentina.

15

7

CHANGE THE COLOUR OF A FUNCTION

You may remember that the Argentine flag has two colours and three rectangles, so you will have to change the colour of the second function. Click on the `set color to` block of the second function you created in Step 6 and choose the white colour.

Change the function name from 'Rectangle blue2' to 'Rectangle white'.

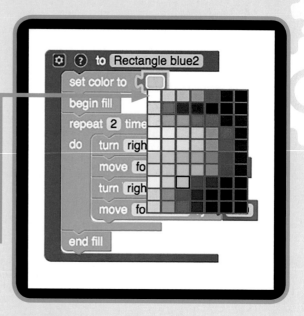

8

DRAW A FLAG USING FUNCTIONS

Leave the functions on one side of the white canvas and add the following blocks beneath the Rectangle blue block you created at the end of Step 5, using the Turtle and Functions menus. Remember, purple blocks are found in the Functions menu; light green blocks in the Turtles menu.

Press ▶ Run to test your program.

Did you know?

Located on the border between Argentina and Brazil, Iguazú Falls are the largest waterfall system in the world. Iguazú is a series of 275 waterfalls, which fall a distance of 75 metres.

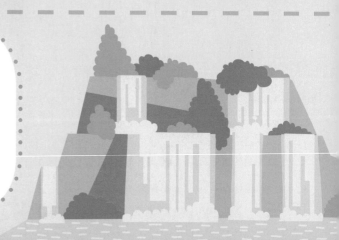

9 ADD A COLOURED MESSAGE

Let's add a message in coloured text.
Add the following block to your program:

This message will appear above the flag.

The font size will automatically be set to 14, but you can change it to any size you want.

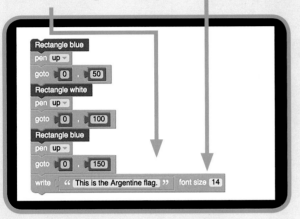

Press ▶ Run to test your program.

CHALLENGE

Use your Python writing skills and the facts you have read in this project to add information about Argentina to your program. Try placing the facts in different places on the screen.

TROUBLESHOOTING

If the message: 'This is the Argentine flag.' is not right above the flag, change the co-ordinates in these blocks:

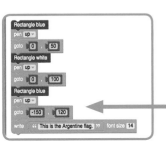

Did you know?

Luciana Aymar is a retired Argentine field hockey player. She is the only player in history to receive the Player of the Year Award eight times and she is considered to be one of the best female hockey players of all time.

10 ADD TEXT

Now we can add some facts using 'print' blocks from the Text menu:

These lines will appear separately at the bottom of the screen.

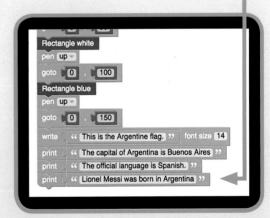

Press ▶ Run to test your program.

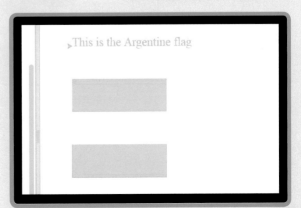

POPPY FLOWER

IT'S TIME FOR SOME FLOWER POWER!

You're going to draw a poppy using functions and loops.

Poppies come in many different colours, such as white, pink, yellow, orange, red or blue.

1 GETTING STARTED

Go to Trinket:
https://trinket.io/ and log in.

Type in your username and password.

2

OPEN A NEW TRINKET

Click on **New Trinket ▼** and click on Blocks.

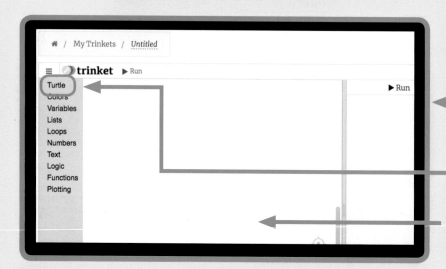

⬅ You will see the following window.

⬅ Click on Turtle.

You will drop the blocks for your program in this white canvas.

From the Turtle menu, select `shape turtle ▾` . Click on the drop-down menu and select 'circle'. We will use a circle to create our flower pattern.

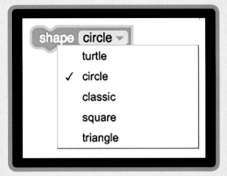

Did you know?
The Golden Poppy, or California Poppy, is the Californian State Flower. It grows wild throughout California and became the state flower in 1903. .

CODE!

You can draw your poppy using lots of different circles.

Did you know?
Every year, on 11 November, people remember the end of the First World War. The common field poppy has become a symbol of this remembrance, because these poppies began to grow in the fields of battle when the war had ended.

3 WRITE IN PYTHON

Add this block to your program:

Press `▶ Run` to test your program. You should see a large circle on the right of your screen.

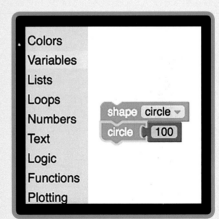

4 MAKE A PETAL

The circle has no colour inside and it is a bit big for the screen. Let's fix this by adding the following blocks to your program:

Change this number by clicking inside the box and typing over the old number with the new one.

Press ▶ Run to test your program.

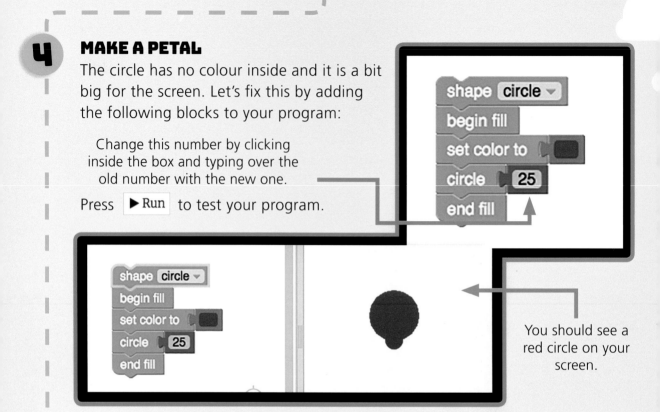

You should see a red circle on your screen.

5 CREATE A FUNCTION

Click on Functions and add the block to your program.

6 NAME THE FUNCTION

It is important to name the function so you know what you can do with it. Click inside the box which says 'do something', delete and type 'Petal'. After that, click on Functions again and you will see a block called 'Petal'. This is the function you have just created.

From now on, every time you want to draw a petal, you will only need to use the function 'Petal'.

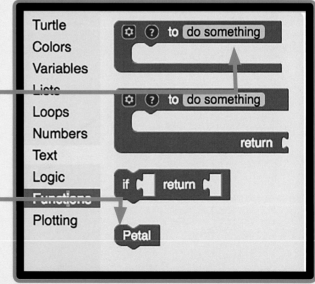

USE LOOPS

A poppy has four petals. Programmers can use loops to repeat the same instruction many times. Add the following code to your program, using the Functions, Loops and Turtle menus:

Press ▶Run to test your program.

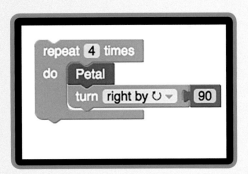

You should see a red flower on the right of your screen.

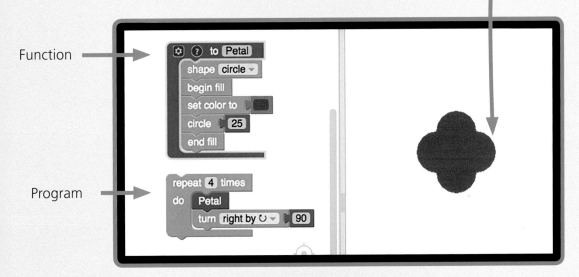

Function →

Program →

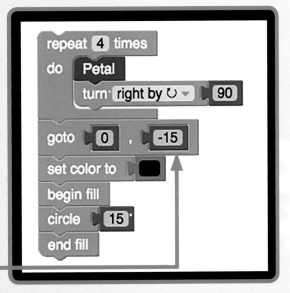

8

CREATE THE CENTRE

You will have to add another circle to make the centre of the flower. This time the circle will be black. Add the following blocks to your program:

Press ▶Run to test your program.

This position block will place the black circle right on the centre of the flower.

ADD THE STEM

To finish your flower, you need to add the stem. Add the following blocks to your program to finish the poppy:

This block will make the program continue drawing. Remember to use the drop-down menu to select down.

Press ▶ Run to test your program.

Your program should look like this:

This block will make the program stop drawing.

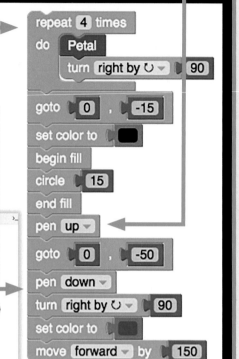

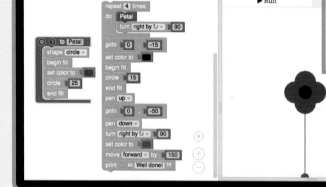

10 USE TEXT BLOCKS

In Trinket, you can use Text blocks to write a message at the bottom of your screen.

Use these two blocks to write your message.

Press ▶ Run to test your program.

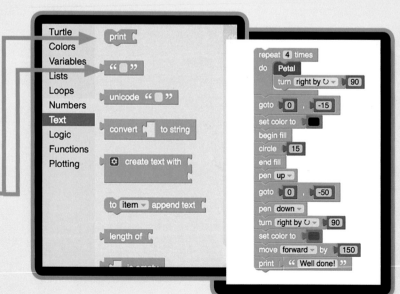

TROUBLESHOOTING

If the petals are too small, you need to change the size of the circle in the function.

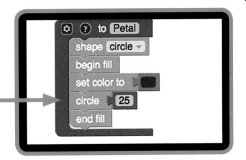

Did you know?

The Bluebonnet Poppy is the state flower of Texas. They are easily found in fields and along roadsides throughout central and southern Texas.

CHALLENGE

Use your knowledge about functions to create a Golden Poppy (see page 20) and a Bluebonnet Poppy (see above). Use the `set color to` block to change the poppy's colour and the `circle 20` block to change the petals' size.

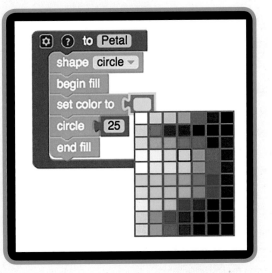

THE CATERPILLAR
GET READY FOR CREEPY CRAWLY FUN!

READY >>

You're going to create a program using variables and loops to draw a caterpillar.

Did you know?
A caterpillar is the larva of a moth or butterfly. Caterpillars eat a lot of food before producing a hard, outer shell called a chrysalis. Inside the chrysalis, the caterpillar develops into a moth or butterfly.

1 GETTING STARTED
Go to Trinket: https://trinket.io/ and log in.

Type in your username and password.

The life cycle of a butterfly

1. Egg
The female lays lots of little round eggs and attaches them to leaves or stems.

2. Caterpillar (or larva)
The eggs develop into caterpillars.

3. Chrysalis (often called the pupa)
This is a rest stage in which the caterpillar develops a hard, outer case. Inside the chrysalis, the caterpillar changes and becomes a butterfly.

4. Butterfly
Once the butterfly is ready to emerge, the case around the chrysalis splits open.

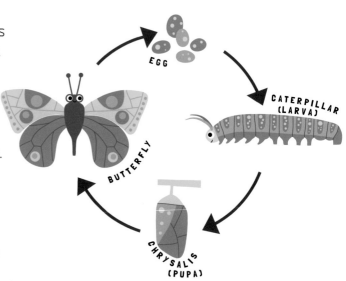

2 **OPEN A NEW TRINKET**

Click on New Trinket ▼ and click on Turtle.

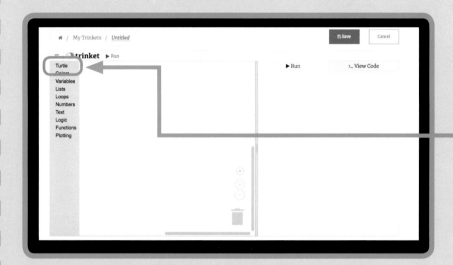

Click on Turtle.

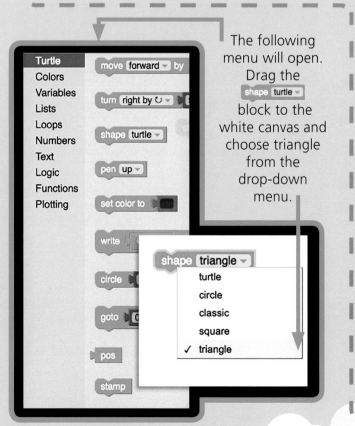

The following menu will open. Drag the `shape turtle` block to the white canvas and choose triangle from the drop-down menu.

A variable is a space in the computer memory where you can store information such as numbers, text, or lists of numbers and text. To create a variable you need to name it.

CODE! ≫

Turtle
Colors
Variables
Lists
Loops
Numbers
Text

Create variable...

3 CREATE VARIABLES

Click on the Variables menu
and then select `Create variable...`

The following message will appear at the top of the screen:

New variable name:

|

Cancel   OK

Type 'set to', and click OK.
'set to' is the name of the
variable and it will appear in the
Variables menu, like this: →

set (set to ▾) to ▮

set to ▾

Add two more variables: one named x and the other named y.

4

Co-ordinates in
programming
are the number
of pixels (each
small block of
colour which
forms a picture)
across the screen
(horizontally)
and the number
of pixels down
(vertically).

USE VARIABLES

Drag and drop the `set set to ▾ to` block from the Variables menu under the shape block. Click on the drop-down menu and choose x.

Then go to the Numbers menu, select and drag the first block into your program and type in 150.

Add another two blocks from the Turtle menu to your program: →

shape [triangle ▾]
set [x ▾] to [
   set to
✓ x
  y
  Rename variable...

This variable will make
the triangle move along
the screen horizontally.

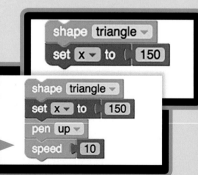

shape [triangle ▾]
set [x ▾] to (150)

shape [triangle ▾]
set [x ▾] to (150)
pen [up ▾]
speed [10]

Did you know?
A caterpillar has up to 4,000
muscles in its body

5 CREATE A LIST USING LOOPS

Click on the Loops menu and drag
this block on to the white canvas:

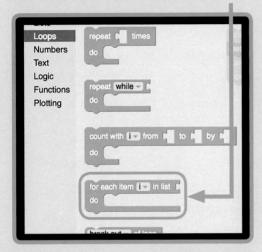

Now go to the Lists menu
and select the 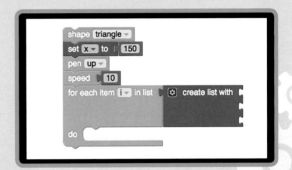 create list with

block. Your program should
look like this:

6 ADD ITEMS TO THE LIST

A caterpillar's body is made of several parts.
The list you created in the previous step
will help you add parts of the body to your
drawing. Click on ⚙ in the
create list with block to add items.

You have to drag the item block and drop
it inside the list block in the pop-out list.
Add item until you have six inside the list
block. The items will appear as six jigsaw
slots in the create list with block.

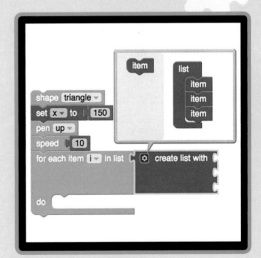

Did you know?
Most caterpillars are shades of green
or brown and are relatively hairless, but
some caterpillars are very hairy and
often brightly coloured.

7 ADD COLOUR TO THE LIST

Click on the Colors menu and drag and drop the red colour box into each of the items on the list. Click inside each red block and choose a different colour for each part of the caterpillar's body.

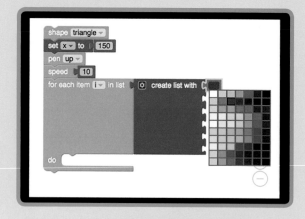

To add a new colour box to the list, right-click on the red block and select Duplicate.

8 DRAW THE CATERPILLAR'S BODY

Now you need to draw the items in the list. You will use circles to draw the caterpillar's body. Add the following blocks from the Turtle, Numbers (blue blocks) and Variables menus:

This block will set the colour for the items in the list.

This block will make the program start on the right of the screen.

Each 'stamp' will be one of the legs of the caterpillar.

This variable will move each new circle to the left.

Press ▶ Run to test your program. You should see the caterpillar's body on your screen.

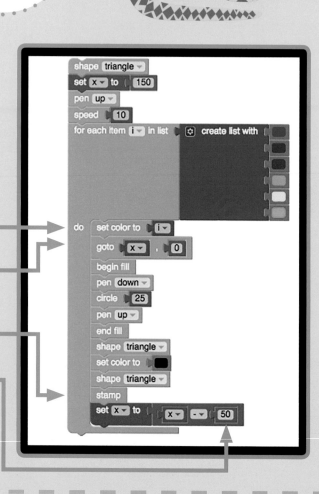

9 DRAW THE CATERPILLAR'S HEAD

Add the following blocks to your program:

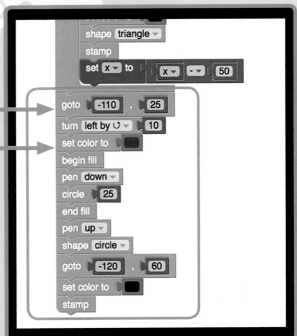

This block will position the caterpillar's head.

Choose any suitable colour for your caterpillar's head.

Press ▶ Run to test your program.

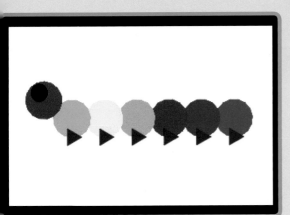

Did you know?

Caterpillars are eating machines! They love eating nettles, wild grasses and flowers. During the first stage of their lives – the larval stage – caterpillars can eat 27,000 times their own weight!

TROUBLESHOOTING

If the circles that make the body of the caterpillar are a bit separated, you can solve this by reducing the number in the variable.

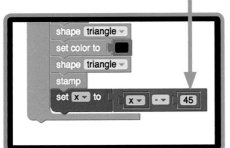

CHALLENGE

Use your knowledge of drawing circles to draw an orange or an apple next to the caterpillar. Remember, they are always hungry!

GLOSSARY

Canvas
An area of the screen for drawing on.

Co-ordinates
The position of a pixel on the screen.
It is the number of pixels across
the screen (x axis/horizontally)
and the number of pixels down
(y axis/vertically).

Function
A set of instructions that can be used to
do an action.

Loop
An instruction or set of instructions that
keep repeating.

Pixel
A point on the screen. It is the smallest
dot the computer is capable of drawing.

Turtle
An image that shows the position of
the program on the white canvas.

Variable
A place to store data in a computer
program. It has a name and a value.

FURTHER INFORMATION

BOOKS

Kids Get Coding by Heather Lyons and Elizabeth Tweedale (Wayland, 2016)

Generation Code: I am a Python Programmer by Max Wainewright (Wayland, 2017)

WEBSITES

https://trinket.io/

https://www.python.org/

INTERNET SAFETY

The Internet is a great resource, which helps you connect, communicate and be creative.

However, you need to stay safe online. Always remember:

1. If you see anything online which makes you feel uncomfortable or unhappy, tell a grown up straight away.

2. Never share your personal information, such as your full name, address or date of birth, with anybody online.

3. Remember that people online may not always be who they say they are. Never share anything with people online unless you are sure you know who they are.

NOTE TO PARENTS

It is advisable to:

- Use filtering software to block unwanted content

- Familiarise yourself with the privacy settings of your device

- Set up passwords to protect personal information.

INDEX

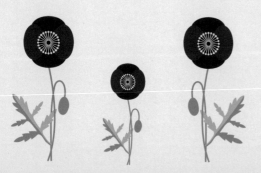